TEXAS IS THE REASON:

FIVE DECADES OF THE TEXAS CHAINSAW MASSACRE

BY TIM MURR

TEXAS IS THE REASON:

FIVE DECADES OF THE TEXAS CHAINSAW MASSACRE

BY TIM MURR

St Rooster Books 2022

No part of this book may be reproduced without the written consent of the author except in the case of review. This book is a long form critical essay on the *Texas Chainsaw Massacre* and related media. St Rooster Books makes no claim of ownership on anything besides the words written herein.

Contact

Holyrooster76 @ gmail.com

Follow St Rooster on Twitter

@st_roosterbooks

Dedicated to Tobe

CONTENTS

THE MAD AND THE MACABRE

1974

1983

1986

1990

1991

1995

2003

2005

2013

2015

2017

2022

PRECURSORS, RELATIVES, AND KNOCK OFFS

HORROR IS MY LIFE

THE MAD AND MACABRE

The original 1974 *The Texas Chainsaw Massacre* is deservedly revered as not just a classic horror film or one of the great proto-slasher films, but as a testament to savage American art. From the opening text crawl and ominous voice over telling us that what we are about to experience is a true story, to the unrelentingly grim documentary-like shooting style, to Marilyn Burns' unending scream through the second half of the film, *TCM* still holds a power over viewers. Regardless of how sophisticated special effects became in the ensuing years, or how much gore we've been treated to, it holds a power to not lose its bite despite how desensitized we, the viewer, may have become after more than 40 years living on a horror diet. The film spawned eight sequels, none of which have been particularly successful from a critical or financial perspective, a few comic book series, a couple of video game appearances, and many toys. As a franchise, *TCM* doesn't have much in common with *Friday the 13th, Halloween*, or *A Nightmare on Elm Street*. Sequels weren't churned out almost yearly and Leatherface, though the only real constant character through the series, isn't the same type of unstoppable killing machine, though obviously he's a tough son of a bitch and survivor. Director Tobe Hooper didn't give us a sequel until 1986 with Part II, a gore-soaked black comedy that featured Dennis Hopper as a rogue Texas Ranger hunting the Sawyer family across the state. The film was a bomb, somehow (and it honestly confuses me, because I adore Part II) and its distributor, Canon, sold the rights to the studio Freddy Kreuger built: New Line Cinema.

In 1989, at the age of 13, I was still very much of two minds. That year, Tim Burton's *Batman* had come out and I thought it was one of the greatest things I'd ever seen (despite some misgivings about giving the Joker an origin story, barely showing Batman in suit, and no Robin at all). Then on the other hand, I'd been exploring horror for about two years or so, starting with *Tales from the Darkside* in syndication and then stumbling on to a double feature of *Halloween II* and *Night of the Living Dead* on Halloween of 1987, the same year I got my first issue of *Fangoria* and the year *Halloween IV; The Return of Michael Myers* came out. So, at 13, I was as committed to horror as I was to the comic book superheroes I'd loved for as far back as I could remember. With horror I had my limits. I had no problems with Jason, Freddy, or Michael, but I was wary of the Cenobites. I'd seen some clips from *Hellraiser* and found even a small dose of that world too overwhelming. The other big one missing from my viewing experience was *Texas Chainsaw Massacre*. I had been forbidden by my stepdad from watching that one. He had no problem letting me rent *Friday the 13th* and *Dawn of the Dead* over and over, but *TCM* was off limits. It was just too sick, too awful. 'I wasn't ready for it.' I took him at his word, because when I was 12, I caught *Henry: Portrait of a Serial Killer* on late night cable. I wasn't ten minutes into the film before I knew I had made a mistake, that this film was beyond me, and I really should not have been watching it. *Night of the Living Dead* had blown my mind the year before with its nihilistic closing moments-*Henry* opened with nihilism and never relented for a moment. I was shaking by the time the movie was over. It was the middle of the night, my room was in the basement, and I didn't get any sleep until the sun came up.

So, my perception was that *TCM* would go beyond what I was ready to experience, I wasn't even going to bother with it. And then the greatest movie trailer I'd seen came out...We start with soft music and a tree by a lake. The camera pans to the right and settles on a husky man looking out contemplatively over the lake, and a voice over tells us, "Some tales are told and soon forgotten. But a legend is forever..." Then a silver chainsaw starts rising out of the water, held by a woman's hand and is thrown into the air. The man catches it and holds it aloft, King Arthur style and it's struck by lightning. He spins around, revs the engine to screams of horror, as the camera zooms in on his horrible "face," and we are told "now the real terror begins." The film was, of course, *Leatherface: Texas Chainsaw Massacre III*. The first time I saw that trailer, I sat back laughing and said, "whoa! That's fucking cool!" The trailer also announced that the film was produced by the people behind *A Nightmare on Elm Street,* and I recognized the New Line Cinema logo right away. I was sold.

Although I can't find a video of it online, I remember there being a set report, and maybe some of the info I knew about the behind-the-scenes controversy came from *Fangoria*, but at any rate, I knew before seeing the film that the producers were coming down hard on director Jeff Burr and screenwriter David J Schow to tone down the violence in the film. They wanted an R-rating, but what Schow had written was well into X-rated territory and in fact, that's what the MPAA gave the initial cut of the film. There was no way I was ever going to get to see it in theaters and I would have to wait for the VHS to come out, but since that was released uncut, it was no skin off my nose.

While waiting for my local video store to get *Leatherface* in, I was faced with the fact that there were still two films in the series that I should probably watch first. I had my own video rental membership card, which had no limitations on R-rated movies. As strict as my house was when it came to certain films or heavy metal, I had little parental oversight. Sure, if I got caught listening to Iron Maiden or watching a "dirty movie," I'd catch hell, but I'd have to be noticed first, so if I was sly, I could get away with a great number of things. So, one weekend, I get *Dawn of the Dead* and *Day of the Dead* again (I rented both of those films so many times, one weekend after another) and I grabbed the first *TCM*, with some trepidation. The crude, cartoonish VHS box art was something I'd stopped in front of many times. It featured Leatherface in a suit and tie, running at you with his chainsaw, with a huge closeup of a woman's face taking up the background. "The most horrifying motion picture I have ever seen," critic Rex Reed was quoted at the top of the box, while on the back was a grainy still of Leatherface carrying a poor woman towards an ominously hung meat hook. Holy shit. I was really shaking. This movie was going to be so fucked up!

    The clerk didn't care what I was getting. I was known. I always rented horror movies, but I expected there to be some push back with *TCM*. "Hey, kid, you shouldn't get this one." But no. They let me have it without so much as a raised eyebrow. I got in the car and when asked what I'd gotten, I said, "*Dawn* and *Day of the Dead* and *A Nightmare on Elm Street Part 3*."

    "Again? Why do you keep watching the same movies repeatedly?"

    "I don't know...I just like them."

    A shrug of the shoulders and I had gotten away with it.

1974

The Texas Chainsaw Massacre was released in 1974. It was directed by Tobe Hooper, who had co-written the screenplay with Kim Henkel. The shoot had been notoriously torturous, down in the Texas summer heat, with long hours, real on-set injuries, and star Marilyn Burns truly being pushed to mental breakdown. Hooper assembled a rag tag group of local talent and shot guerrilla style for up to 16 hours a day in consistent 100-degree heat. The smells were horrifying in that farmhouse. People tell stories of that shoot like they'd been to war.

The film opens with an ominous voiceover from Night Court's John Larroquette, telling us this was a true story. Which was as scary as it was bull shit. The Texas Chainsaw Massacre was not a true story but was loosely based on one of the most famous and ghoulish American crime cases, the saga of Ed Gein. Ed Gein had been a grave robber, who fashioned clothing and furniture out of the dead bodies he dug up. He also murdered two local women and kept their remains at his house. What the police found in Gein's home was horrifying beyond belief. He'd made bowls out of skulls, had lamp shades and wastebaskets made of skin, a belt of nipples, human skin leggings, and skin masks, among several other things. He was deemed insane and died in a mental institution. The case was so shocking, the news reverberated across the country and inspired a writer by the name of Robert Bloch to write one of the most famous horror novels of all time, which was in turn made into one of the most famous horror movies of all time, *Psycho*. The case would also go on to inspire Thomas Harris's "Buffalo Bill" in his landmark novel, *The Silence of the Lambs*, which itself was turned into a landmark film. And there were others along the way, like 1974's *Deranged: Confessions of a Necrophile*, from Alan Ormsby (*Children Shouldn't Play with Dead Things, Popcorn, Cat People*), a stab at telling the true story, but a wonky pacing diffuses the overall experience, but when the film works, it really works. There are a couple of exploitative biopics as well.

So, while *TCM* was far from a true story, Hooper and Henkel did get some things straight from Gein's story. Some of which were greatly toned down, while other things were ratcheted up to horrific degrees, the cannibalism, for example. Bull shit or not, that opening crawl and voiceover are incredibly effective and chilling. No matter how many times I've watched the film over the years, I still get that same uneasy feeling in my gut as the opening credits roll which cuts to that sun baked close up of a corpse's face and that slow pull back, revealing the desecration of a grave, with a corpse propped up on a tombstone. Hooper and Henkel draw a line in the fucking sand in less than ten minutes. Sure, you could spend all day listing films with great openings, but we're talking about a particular strand of savage American art that few films really represent-James McNaughton achieves that status with *Henry* and Sam Peckinpah does it with *Straw Dogs*.

Texas Chainsaw Massacre, for all its reputation as a gritty, docu-style, freakish, horror show is really like a Greek tragedy, as we follow a doomed group of travelers while they descend unknowingly into Hell. Yes, those other elements are there, but we're not going to let them be negatives. Unlike many later slasher films that would introduce us to a cast of two-dimensional walking clichés to be handily dispatched by a masked maniac, *TCM* takes its time introducing us to Sally, her invalid brother Franklin, and their friends-Jerry, Kirk, and Pam. They're just five normal teenagers on a weekend trip to check on Sally and Franklin's grandfather's grave, which happens to be in the same cemetery as the desecrations. We're told in the opening that this group is doomed. Rather than that knowledge spoiling any twists and turns, Hooper and Henkel don't bother trying to be clever-they don't have to be, they're approach is a challenge. 'This is what we're going to show you,' is pretty much a dare to keep us watching. And of course, we do! The tension isn't not knowing what happens, but how it happens. Compare it to another important proto slasher also released in 1974, Bob Clark's *Black*

Christmas. We never really know the motivation of the killer, Billy, as he stalks a group of sorority sisters in their own home, who the killer is, or who might survive. This was a far more, true template for future slashers, as we saw four years later with John Carpenter's *Halloween* and two years after that with Sean Cunningham's *Friday the 13th*. *Texas Chainsaw Massacre* doesn't wait until the closing moments to finally unmask the killer and give us some handy exposition (nor does *Black Christmas*, but the cliché still holds), but rather continues to show its cards, seep every frame in grit and grime and an ominous tone, and by around the halfway point we've got a pretty damn good idea of what's going on and then it just keeps going. Another notable difference, Leatherface and his family aren't stalking their victims. The victims keep coming to their damn house.

    I envy everyone who watches *TCM* for the first time, even if they hate it in the end, there's no denying that they've experienced something-a piece of art that demanded their attention, something that can't be shrugged off or disregarded. I vividly remember getting home from the video store and going straight to my room, which was in the corner of our basement and had no windows, so when the lights were off, it was pitch black. I had a little tv and little second-hand VCR, that didn't have a fast forward or record button. I shut the door and put a 2x4 under the nob (because I didn't have a lock) and popped the tape in. The movie was so damn strange. After the crawl and voice over we get a black screen and then a date of August 18, 1973. The screen stays black, and we hear digging and panting, and then a flashbulb reveals parts of dead bodies in extreme closeup. Finally, the voice over of a newscaster and an extreme closeup of a rotting skull in an ominous orange dawn. Followed by a title card and opening credits on over-exposed video of the sun and the voiceover continues, running down a list of tragic news stories. It feels as apocalyptic as the opening of George Miller's *The Road Warrior*, but more hopeless. Our protagonists arrive at the cemetery, which is crawling with gawkers and concerned family members checking on loved ones' resting places. We have a doomsayer there, but he's nowhere as coherent as Crazy Ralph in the original *Friday the 13th*. He's drunk and sprawled out in a spare tire, and no one seems to care. You almost feel like there's been some other greater event that these sun dazed spectators are survivors of.

    This world Hooper guides us into is a funhouse mirror reflection of America in the 1970s. The summer of love, the age of the hippies, had come to an end with the brutal Tate/La Bianca murders carried out by a cult under the sway of Charles Manson and a Rolling Stones concert in Altamont, California ended in the violent death of a black fan at the hands of the Hell's Angels biker gang, who had been hired as security. Of course, we can't forget to mention the police violence at the Democratic National Convention-an event so traumatizing Hunter S Thompson still struggled to write about it decades later. The assassinations of Martin Luther King and Malcolm X and John and Robert Kennedy horrified and angered the nation. There were riots. Cities burned. The country was exploding. And above it all loomed the Vietnam War, a manufactured debacle of aggression in the name of fighting the Red Menace of Communism. And then we lost. Retreated. There was an oil crisis that resulted in lines at the pump miles long. The struggle for Civil Rights for not only Black America, but for gays, women, and Native Americans continued to rage. President Nixon was exposed for the corrupt, monstrous bastard he had always been, and the tentacles of a new conservatism started to wrap themselves around the Republican Party, dressed in the guise of Christianity, which would lead to the Moral Majority coup of the 1980s and the election of the doddering puppet Ronald Reagan. *The Texas Chainsaw Massacre* is a microcosm or a pure distillation of all of that. An economy laid waste by automation, leaving working people to starve and go mad and resort to extreme measures of survival, with only capitalism surviving as a last means of order. Where in some post-apocalyptic films fuel or water are precious commodities and currency, here it is meat. The Sawyer clan came from the beef industry, the slaughterhouse. When mechanisms took away their jobs, they switched the type of meat they survived and profited off.

You could also read in a Haves and Have Nots storyline here as well. Sally and her friends may not be rich, but they have a van, they have free time, they don't seem destitute, and so far, Jerry and Kirk haven't been drafted. They roll into a devastated area for a good reason but take time to look at the freakshow local yokels, visit Sally and Franklin's grandparents' house, and look for a place to go swimming. Quite a striking difference from the way the Sawyers are living, picking off travelers to make human BBQ to sell the other economic captives of their little corner of Nowhere, Texas and to keep their own bellies full. They're working people, sweating it out from sunup to sundown. (Going back to the idea that there was some cataclysmic event that had recently occurred, Sally and Franklin are still fairly young, and they had spent a lot of time growing up at their grandparents' place, and yet when they arrive, the house is a burned-out shell being reclaimed by nature. This film offers layer after layer of subtext, and I love to get lost in it.)

There are no safe spaces in Sawyer America. If you're not manning the grill, then you're meat. Jerry and Kirk are nice guys, but they're probably not used to being anything less than casual alpha males, but without even knowing it, they expose their whole group to their first brush with danger, when they stop to give a hitchhiker, aka The Hitchhiker, aka Nubbins Sawyer, a ride, because they feel bad for the man, when they see him limping down the road in the pulverizing Texas heat. Nubbins is even more strange than the drunk in the spare tire, back at the cemetery. He has physical maledictions, a speech impediment, and he's wired like a meth head. He claims to have been at the old slaughterhouse where he and his family used to work, but later we find out that he was responsible for the macabre corpse art and grave desecrations. Nubbins keeps trying to get the group to drive him all the way to his house and to buy one of his Polaroids. Their good deed does not go unpunished, and Nubbins attacks the nearly helpless Franklin with Franklin's own pocket-knife. Jerry and Kirk throw Nubbins out of the van, which Nubbins marks with Franklin's blood. The group is so sure of the otherwise goodness of the world, that they continue to the Hardesty place, rather than just getting the hell out of Dodge, never realizing that the hunt is on and they're nothing but cattle, doomed and bound for the cooking flames. (Side note, I wonder if the personal make-up of the group was a nod to *Scooby Doo, Where Are You?* You've got five friends in a green van, two guys and two girls, and poor Franklin has no one to pair off with and winds up being the grating comic relief. No? Ok, moving on.) They're next brush with danger is when they arrive at a roadside gas station and BBQ stand. There's no gas, maybe later, but not at the moment, so logically they shouldn't drive further out of their way, because they're doing nothing but running the risk of being out of gas in the middle of nowhere, but they continue to trust that the world is ok and that there will be gas in the future and getting to the old swimming hole is worth it anyway. Even the cook at the gas station warns them to stay away from that old house, but youthful folly and sage advice rarely dance together. So, they buy some BBQ and head on down the road. And we the helpless viewer sink a little lower into our seat because that's one more step towards the hulking beast in a skin mask we saw on the back of the VHS box.

  I've got no intention of recapping a nearly fifty-year-old film you've likely seen, but it's safe to say that the moment they arrive at the grandparent's home, the group has crossed an imaginary boundary, or maybe more appropriately an invisible boundary, when and where the world they once knew is gone and unattainable. That sunburned highway is their River Styx and they've arrived in Hell. There's no electricity. There's no water in the swimming hole, the gas is too far away, and the only hope lies in the heart of the spider web. Its Kirk and Pam that discover the Sawyer house, after finding that the swimming hole is nothing but a dusty hole in the ground. They try knocking, to see if they can buy some gas from the owners, but when there's no answer Kirk lets himself inside, while Pam waits on the swing in the yard.

There are no more brushes with danger, danger is within reach and it's all around. The house is madness, decorated with the bones of meals past. A symbol of Heartland America, the big white farmhouse, something that should be comforting, and a welcome sight, becomes a waking charnel nightmare. Kirk is horrified, but reacts too slowly, his fight or flight response isn't attuned to this harsh and unexpected shift in reality. Before he can retreat from the house, the final nail in their coffin appears. The man the box art promised, Leatherface.

When Leatherface suddenly fills the doorway before Kirk and raises his hammer over his head, it sucks the air out of the room. That moment never fails to make me gasp, I can't help it. Leatherface is unlike anything in cinema before and nothing has compared since. A big brute in a skin mask and apron, we can't see his eyes through the darkened sockets. His earth tone clothes create a striking contrast against the blood red wall adorned with animal skulls behind him. This scene looks especially amazing in the 4k restoration released by Dark Sky Films. The sound design around Leatherface bringing the hammer down on to Kirk's head, Kirk hitting the ground, and spasming on the walkway, followed by that earth-shattering steel door slam is a huge component to why this scene is so potently terrifying.

So now we are through the looking glass. We follow Pam's ass (literally) into the web, looking for Kirk and that's when the real madness begins. Seeing the house through Pam's eyes isn't something that previous cinematic experiences prepared us for. Not Luis Bunel's *An Andalusian Dog*, not Tod Browning's *Freaks*, not Sam Peckinpah's *Wild Bunch*. Hooper creates a kaleidoscope of terror punctuated by Leatherface's frantic discovery of yet another interloper in his home. From chasing her out the door, to roughly catching her on the porch and carrying her into the kitchen, to slamming her writhing and very conscious body on a meat hook, and finally to Leatherface wildly searching the house for any other outsiders, *The Texas Chainsaw Massacre* becomes a golden standard in horror.

In all fairness, I think I need to talk about Wes Craven's 1972 directorial debut *Last House on the Left*. In everything I've talked about above, Hooper crafts his horror through sleight of hand. He tricks us into believing we're seeing something more graphic than we are, but even Pam being impaled on the meat hook is completely bloodless and not even in camera even though we're looking right at it. Hooper even went to the MPAA and asked how he could do the meat hook gag and still get a PG rating (he couldn't, they told him). Craven was unbound by sense of "getting away with it," I suppose? Inspired by Ingmar Bergman's *The Virgin Spring*, Craven crafted an explicit, horrifying, disturbing, and haunting picture about the brutal rape and torture of two teenage girls and the subsequent revenge sought by one of the girl's parents. On the outside, *Last House* sounded like some nasty exploitation thing, like *I Drink Your Blood* or something by Al Adamson or Herschell Gordon Lewis. The problem was that Craven was far more intelligent, literate, and perhaps sensitive to violence than either of them and brought a level of violence that went beyond the cartoonish nature of *Blood Feast* and subjected the audience to something much more realistic and psychologically damaging. When we're talking about the birth of modern horror, where everything that has happened in the last fifty years starts, first we talk about George A Romero's *Night of the Living Dead*, then it's Craven's *Last House*, and after those it's *TCM* and Bob Clark's *Black Christmas*. They're the biggest, most often cited, and most influential horror films of the modern era. *Last House* is the only one that I think is scarier and more disturbing than *TCM* (for me personally, this is an opinion piece, not a definitive line in the sand), but I don't think it's a better movie. In fact, I haven't been able to make myself go back and re-watch since I saw it at age 12. It's one of three films I watched at that age, the other two being *I Spit on Your Grave* and *Henry; Portrait of a Serial Killer*, that I never had a desire to re-watch (although, thanks to Joe Bob Briggs, I did finally watch *Henry* again). *Last House* puts the viewer through the wringer. Craven was not a violent man and was not enamored with seeing acts of violence on screen. He didn't think violence should be exciting, that it should be disturbing. So, he made it disturbing. He left no room for living vicariously through cartoonish monsters. You needed to hurt. Compare that to *TCM*, for all its squirm inducing hysteria, its nightmare *Alice in Wonderland* aesthetics, it's still a highly watchable film with a high re-watch value. It has the black humor of a fun house ride that balances the depressing, bleak nihilism of the world it portrays. *Last House* is just nihilism and even though the parents exact their revenge against the killers, there's no sense of justice at the end, no closure. Violence begets tragedy and there may not be room for anything else in a post Manson, post Viet Nam world. It's even more grim than Ben surviving the *Night of the Living Dead* just to be shot in the head. After all, look at that film's sequels, maybe Ben was one of the lucky ones. *TCM* ends with a screaming/laughing Marilyn Burns riding away from a funhouse in hell into the rising sun, while Leatherface does an interpretive chainsaw dance of defeat and bewilderment. It's a weird, absurdist twist to end on, and even though the "bad guys" weren't punished for their crimes, the viewer doesn't feel cheated.

TCM is a rollercoaster that scares the shit out of you in the moment and when it's over you can't wait to ride again. *Last House* is a cruel act that breaks your heart. (And it's weird in hindsight, that Craven's first two films, the other being *The Hills Have Eyes*, which probably borrowed more than just *TCM*'s set designer, are such hardcore, angry, nihilistic films, when Craven himself was such a sweet, intelligent, and soft-spoken man.) Ok, this long-winded digression is about my point that there was nothing in cinema prior to *TCM* to prepare you for the journey Hooper and Henkel takes you on, knowing that *Last House* and Lewis's *2000 Maniacs* and *The Wizard of Gore* existed. *TCM* was a bigger film than any of them and was of a much higher quality in terms of writing, directing, set design, and characters. This is even more evident when you view the 4k restoration. It crackles with energy and was ahead of its time. It has a sophistication hidden behind its skin mask. *Last House* has a sophistication too, basically being a Bergman remake, but the sensitive mind behind it is washed away in the film's pure negativity. In other words, it's not a ride I want to go on again.

So, between where I left off and where Leatherface is left bizarrely dancing on the side of the road while Sally escapes, Sally and Franklin find themselves alone with a van they can't drive and a house that can't provide shelter. Jerry has disappeared into the dark looking for Kirk and Pam, so the ill-fated siblings are left with no choice but to follow Jerry into the thickets, their very own dry and treacherous entrance to Hades. And worse, Franklin is a millstone around Sally's neck. She's scared and desperate, tired and struggling to push his wheelchair while he whines and complains incessantly, his wheels getting stuck over and over, again. No doubt, the thought crosses her mind to just leave him and come back with Jerry and the others, but then again, he's her brother. Just when their bickering is going to hit a fever pitch, Leatherface bursts into the beam of their flashlight, chainsaw roaring, and this time we do see his eyes inside the skin mask-somehow, that's even scarier and more disturbing.

Sally bears witness to Franklin's awful demise before being pursued blindly through the thickets until she gets back to the BBQ place and into Drayton Sawyer's arms, thinking she's finally found solace, but throwing herself on his mercy earns her a ride in his pickup truck, wrapped in a burlap sack, and being beaten with a broom handle. He drives her back to the Sawyer farm, finding Nubbins returning home and we finally have the whole picture; Nubbins, Drayton, and Leatherface are brothers and soon we'll be introduced the patriarch of the family, "Grampa."

The infamous dinner scene that follows is nerve shredding. Between Sally's screams and the howls and laughter of the Sawyers, it's hard not to wince or turn down your television. The crazy close ups, the ambient noise, the mad dialogue-it's a palatable insanity, partly because its real. That house was 100 degrees, everyone was exhausted, the smells were really like a slaughterhouse. At one point, Gunnar Hansen, the man that played Leatherface, sliced Marilyn Burns' finger open with a real knife to finally get the shot of her bleeding. The first time I saw the dinner scene, which included Sally tied to a chair, Leatherface wearing a suit and his "pretty lady" face, Drayton trying to be the normal one before giving into a giggle fit, and Nubbins turning it up to eleven, I was on my feet pacing around my room. There are so many anxiety inducing elements at work here; from the simple fact that everything must be filthy, and bacteria ridden, to the clear, dark parallel to Lewis Carroll's *Alice in Wonderland's* mad tea party, to, again, the amazing sound design. Then we finally meet Grampa, who we learn in part two is 137 years old. In this film he first appears to me a dried out, mummified corpse in his Sunday best, and then he moves! It's a scarring bit of kinder trauma for me, the thrill-seeking young viewer, putting myself in Sally's place, I found myself asking, 'would I even WANT to survive this?' In the ensuing years since this first viewing, I've watched *TCM* with several people and I always like to check out how others are doing at this point, and most of the time they look uncomfortable.

The chaos only escalates when Sally finally breaks free of her captors and leaps through a window and runs to the road for safety. She first flags down a trucker, and then a pick-up truck, but she's pursued off the property by both Nubbins and Leatherface. Nubbins winds up getting killed by the tractor trailer and Leatherface blunders into sawing into his own leg. The whole scene plays out like a comedy of errors, its total slapstick, but we're still reeling from the surreal dinner scene (which takes place just before dawn apparently, a nod to Grampa's vampirism? He's lived this long on a strictly "liquid" diet, Drayton reveals in part two) so the black humor doesn't play the way Hooper intended it. That's important to keep in mind and it took me years to finally see it, but Hooper meant for *TCM* to be kind of funny. When I read about that later I didn't know if it was supposed to be a joke or what, because that damn movie rattled me so hard, but it did explain why I felt a sense of relief/release when it was finally over, and that I was ready for more right away-a stark difference from how I felt after *Henry, Last House, and I Spit on Your Grave*. Now I can see the Marx Brothers influence in the dinner scene, Drayton is Groucho, Nubbins is Chico, and Leatherface is Harpo. The dropping acid in Hell versions, but still.

TCM is far from the only horror film to hold a mirror up to America and show us how ugly we are or could be. Or perhaps it simply lifts the rug a little higher to show where we've swept the refuse of society. In 2020, you watch that blistering heat on the screen, see a devastated economy, and people losing their fucking minds, you realize what a voice Hooper and Henkel spoke with-powerful enough to transcend time, generations, and presidential administrations without losing its ability to shake, rattle, and roar.

After *TCM*, Kim Henkel kept working in film, wearing various hats as writer, producer, director, and actor, without ever gaining huge mainstream success. Tobe Hooper on the other hand, worked rather steadily in film and television throughout the rest of the 70s and into the 90s, before the projects started to become sparse. His 1976 follow up, *Eaten Alive* could have been a spiritual sequel to *TCM*, dealing with a backwoods madman who ran a sleazy motel and fed his customers to his pet alligator. Hooper came back more polished for his TV debut, a mini-series adaptation of Stephen King's *Salem's Lot*, which still holds up as one of the best King adaptations of all time, with some real kinder trauma for a lot of young people who tuned in. 1981's *The Funhouse* was full of great horror easter eggs, had a bit of a slow burn first half before becoming as much of a carnival ride as the funhouse in the movie itself. His biggest hit though, was 1982's *Poltergeist*, which he directed for Stephen

Spielberg, who served as producer, while he directed *E.T.* up the street. There's a famous rumor that Hooper was just a stand in while Spielberg skirted DGA rules by directing both movies at the same time, but that's just bull shit. One cinematographer started that rumor, and I don't even care enough to look up his fucking name. *Poltergeist* is a beautiful amalgamation of Spielberg and Hooper's styles, so miss me with that crap. Following that, in 1983, Hooper started working on what was at the time called *Tobe Hooper's Return of the Living Dead*, but that project got held up and The Cannon Group came calling with a lucrative three picture deal, which spawned the amazing *Lifeforce* and the rather kid friendly *Invaders From Mars*, but what we're interested in right now is Hooper's long awaited sequel to his savage American cinematic masterpiece, I'm talking about *The Texas Chainsaw Massacre Part 2*.

1983

One thing I have no nostalgia for is classic video games, particularly the old Commodore, Intelevision, or Atari games. Sure, as a kid, I could spend up to half an hour playing *Pac Man* or *Space Invaders* on my Atari 2600, but video games never really captured my imagination until I started playing *Grand Theft Auto III* on the Playstation 2. So, I never played the old *Texas Chainsaw* game back in the day, not that my uptight parents would have let me anyway. In fact, I never knew such a thing existed until the toy company NECA released a game deco figure of Leatherface, which was nothing but a plain green figure with a brown head. A huge let down compared to their other game deco figures from *Alien* and *Teenage Mutant Ninja Turtles*.

Not nearly as disappointing as the actual *TCM* game, of course. *Texas Chainsaw Massacre the Game* was developed by Wizard Games, who also made the *Halloween* game around the same time, making them two of the first horror themed video games. *TCM* was a controversial release and some stores refused to carry it, resulting in low sales.

The game play was as incredibly rudimentary, as would be expected. You play as Leatherface chainsawing intruders on to your property. There are no levels, no goals, other than just trying to kill as many people as possible without running out of gas. The environment is reminiscent of *Pitfall*, with cow skulls and wheelchairs as obstacles. Its an odd piece of media, but nothing as cool or fun as the NES *Friday the 13th* game. Fortunately, the future of gaming held much better things for Leatherface.

1986

Hooper wasn't about to let the humor go overlooked for his return to the world of The Sawyers and he also wasn't going to be outdone when it came to blood and gore. This was the 1980s after all, and special effects wizards like Tom Savini, Rick Baker, and Rob Bottin were like rock stars. Yes, the MPAA was cracking down like fascists when it came to horror movies, but there was still plenty of wiggle room for squirm inducing latex and corn syrup gags. Hooper conceived the story with screenwriter Kit Carson and assembled a cast which included Dennis Hopper as Texas Ranger Lefty Enright, the haunted and obsessed uncle of Sally and Franklin, the story's Ahab, Caroline Williams as the rock DJ Stretch, who's looking to break into a real professional career and sees her chance when she accidentally records the Sawyers killing two high school assholes, Bill Johnson, who stepped into the role of Leatherface or Bubba, as he's called throughout the film, and Bill Moseley as Chop Top, Nubbin's twin brother, who's got a metal plate in his head from an injury received while in Viet Nam (Nubbins also features heavily throughout the film, but it's his corpse, which both Leatherface and Chop Top puppet through the film). Most importantly though, Jim Siedow returned to reprise his role as Drayton Sawyer. I really think this was integral to TCM2, as Drayton is sort of the brains of the operation and the face of the family business. Now, fourteen years after the events of the first film, The Sawyers have abandoned their home and turned their BBQ business into a rolling catering service with award winning chili. There's such a great 1980s, "greed is good" sneer to *TCM2*. Hooper really rose to the occasion, going bigger, more outlandish, being louder, and widening the scope of the original film.

We learn in the opening crawl that Sally survived her escape and made it to authorities to tell her mad tale, but months of searching turned up neither the Sawyer house nor any of the victims. *The Texas Chainsaw Massacre* became the stuff of urban legend, but the grizzly killings around the state never stopped. Lefty has been chasing ghosts for fourteen years and has become a bit of a laughingstock among other law enforcement agents. We even get a sense, at the site of the opening killing of the aforementioned high schoolers, as Lefty has shown up to investigate the aftermath, that other cops don't want to know, they want to write it all off as anything but more chainsaw murders. They insist to Lefty it was just some wild kids, even while they are standing over a sawn in half car door, with deep cuts across it.

Roger Ebert, a critic who has famously despised many horror movies of the 80s, called the film "a geek show," and he's not wrong, but I don't see why that must have a negative connotation. The geek show was at one time a side show staple-bums or weirdoes biting the heads off live animals for horrific thrills. Lacking the same depth of cultural relevancy as the original *TCM*, part 2 really is a freak show, as hilarious as it is horrifying. Special effects master Tom Savini was almost as unbound as he ever got to be with Romero's *Dawn* and *Day of the Dead*, but the gags are way wetter and more mean-spirited.

Chop Top alone is a whole freakshow in and of himself. From the plate in his head, the over-the-top pseudo-hippie dialogue, eating his own scalp with a lighter and coat hanger, puppeteering the corpse of his dead twin, Nubbins, to his orgasmic glee when it comes to committing random acts of violence. Chop Top is very indicative of the film's excesses, which Hooper and the cast simply revel in from start to finish.

The film didn't do well upon release. Fans and critics alike were negative as the film was almost nothing like the original film. Gone was the almost-taboo darkness, replaced by an ad campaign that parodied *The Breakfast Club*. The Cannon Group were certainly unhappy, the MPAA was very unhappy and slapped the film with an X rating, but Hooper seemed to simply shrug his shoulders and released the film unrated. It was three films in a row that failed to live up to expectations for Hooper, but looking back at his Cannon output, he gave us three wildly different and wildly entertaining films that I'm happy to return to repeatedly and *TCM2* is the best of the trio.

He could have never caught lightning in a bottle a second time. The elements that created the original film were of their time and moment. It wasn't just story and location, but economic status, and desperation that helped create one of the greatest movies in American cinematic history. It was all still grimy and low budget, of course, but it explodes with all sorts of Splatterpunk glory. It's everything the original was accused of being, but also raised the bar for future sequels, none of which ever even tried to touch part 2's insanity.

Lefty is one of my favorite Dennis Hopper characters. He's nowhere near as unhinged as the photographer in *Apocalypse Now* or Frank Booth in *Blue Velvet*, but as the movie's Ahab, he really is perfect. Hopper comes off as tired and awkward in Lefty's private moments, but slaps on his cowboy hat and summons a big-as-Texas attitude whenever he's in front of others. That classic downfall of men everywhere, the fear of showing vulnerability and going too hard to compensate for inadequacies that come with age and stress. He calls down strength from the Lord Almighty to become God's hand of vengeance as he charges the abandoned theme park, which serves as the new base of operations for the Sawyers, armed with a trio of chainsaws. (I wonder if Hooper was a fan of

Malatesta's Carnival of Blood, which was a carnival with an underground clan of cannibals? Not mention the numerous times *The Joker* used a carnival or sideshow as a hideout.) The only missed opportunity is that we don't get more of Lefty fighting the Sawyers.

You've got three disparate story arcs, loosely intertwining that only really comes together in the final moments of the film. In fact, The Sawyers are barely aware of Lefty at all, even while he's chainsawing the shit out of their hideout. Don't get me wrong, when they finally meet Lefty its very funny and weird, but it would have been nice to have seen Lefty have a go at Leatherface and/or Chop Top earlier in the film, to give the final duel a little more weight.

Caroline Williams owns this movie, though, even up against the stature of Hopper and the scene chewing of Bill Mosely. I feel like Williams' Stretch is a little more than a final girl. She's rowdy and precocious from the start and as soon as she sees an opportunity to get the hell out of the "Heart of Texas" where "there ain't nothing going on," she goes for it without hesitation. She's a rock and roll Lois Lane and sure she needs to be saved by Lefty, because it's a numbers game, with three Sawyers chasing her down in their own labyrinthian hideaway, but once he helps even the odds, she's able to go toe to toe with Chop Top and come out on top.

Needing to recoup some losses, cannon sold the rights to *TCM* to New Line Cinema. And to its credit, New Line was committed to making a hardcore horror film. At the time, the studio would have been getting ready to close the final chapter on their flagship franchise, *A Nightmare on Elm Street*, with 1991s *Freddy's Dead*, but in addition to *TCM*, New Line would also be taking over *Friday the 13th* from Paramount following the box office bomb of 1989s *Jason Takes Manhattan*. In retrospect, that sounds like the making of a modern Universal Pictures monsterverse, but it took two decades to get Freddy and Jason on screen together and New Line was only able to hold on to Leatherface for one film. The results of that film would be a troubled and speedy shoot, tussles with the MPAA, and a director who wanted his name removed from the final product. The steady deluge of sequels based on a handful of seemingly durable characters left in the hands of a mixed bag of directors through the 1980s had started to show enough wear and tear to prove the slasher movie business model was perhaps not so well thought out by the '90s.

1990

Leatherface; The Texas Chainsaw Massacre III is a far different animal than its predecessors. While there's still a streak of black comedy, the overriding tone is much grimmer thanks in large part to a gory and terrifying script by Splatterpunk author David J Schow (*The Crow, Critters 3, Black Leather Required, Negative Burn*). Schow gave Leatherface a new family, keeping only the corpse of Grandpa. Leatherface has seemingly grown up a bit. We find a more confident, sure-footed Leatherface than we've previously seen, he seems less troubled about the doings of the family business, and he's certainly grown into the aggressive nature that would burst out in explosions in the previous movies. *Part III* sets a tone for the subsequent films in that family members become replaceable, and though Kim Henkel returned for *The Next Generation* (1994) and tried to bring Leatherface back to something more recognizable from the first film, we see the other films (a remake, a remake prequel, and a sort of new part two to the original film, and another prequel) really taking the model of *Part III*'s Leatherface. He's quieter, deadlier, and less conflicted about slaughtering people. This isn't a negative for *Leatherface*, but I feel it really hurt the remake and prequel significantly. *Part III* evolves the story, whereas the other two missed the point.

In *Part III*, we join an unmarried couple, Michelle (Kate Hodge) and Ryan (William Butler) driving from Los Angeles to Florida. She's not coming back, and the relationship is strained. Their drive through Texas coincides with the local police's discovery of a horrific body pit full of rotting, mutilated corpses. This scene ups the ante from the original film's opening on a desecrated cemetery and foreshadows the more gruesome turns we have in store. (Blink and you'll miss Caroline Williams reprise her role of Stretch, now a legitimate reporter.) Soon, after hitting an armadillo, the couple pulls over at a gas station where we meet a handsome drifter named Tex (Viggo Mortensen) and a creepy gas station attendant named Alfredo (Tom Everett), who could be an appropriately aged hitchhiker from the first film, down to the Polaroid camera capturing his future dinner. Tex is looking for a ride and trying to help the couple out with a shortcut on a new road that isn't even on their map. When Tex catches Alfredo peaking on Michelle while she's in the bathroom things get crazy, with Alfredo grabbing a shotgun, shooting out the couple's back window, and apparently killing Tex. Michelle and Ryan speed away, taking Tex's route, while Alfredo cackles to himself about the trap being sprung.

As the sun sets, the garage door opens, and a monster truck covered in animal hides pulls out and chases Michelle and Ryan into the desert night. They're able to lose the truck but get a flat tire. After several tense moments of trying to get it changed, Leatherface (R.A. Mihailoff) appears out of the dark and attacks them. They narrowly escape, only to get into an accident with another vehicle being driven by a survivalist named Benny (Ken Foree). Benny tries to help the couple, they warn him of the crazy people chasing them, but he's doubtful of their claims and leaves them on a hillside while he goes for help. Back on the road he's surprised by a tow truck driver that's already on the scene. He has a hook hand, and we quickly begin to be wary of him, as does Benny. The tow truck driver is named Tinker (Joe Unger), and it doesn't take long for us to learn his being there is no accident.

Following another Leatherface attack in the woods, Benny narrowly escapes, but loses Michelle and Ryan, who get separated from each other. Michelle wanders through the woods and comes across a remote house, and we all know who lives there. The house initially seems far more normal than the previous abodes of the Sawyer clan. It's not until Michelle follows a young girl upstairs that we find a room of skeletal remains, and the little girl is a nasty little chip off the old block, stabbing Michelle in the leg. Next, she's caught by Tex, who was part of the trap the whole time. Tinker arrives with an unconscious Ryan, and they're just waiting for Leatherface to arrive with Benny. We see Grandpa's mummified corpse in the kitchen, while Michelle is being tied to a chair with nails driven through her hands. And then we meet the matriarch of the family; Mama (Miriam Byrd-Nethery).

Except for Alfredo being a near perfect stand-in for The Hitchhiker, this version of the family is a stark contrast to the Drayton Sawyer (Jim Siedow) led clan. In the first two films, the family is essentially the same, except Chop Top replacing Nubbins. The quartet of men is loud, wild, unhinged. Emotions are turned way up bordering on cartoonish — or at least oafish. In the original film they seem almost completely detached from the world. In *Part II*, they've learned how to make their family secret (eating folks) into a little family business. The family unit of Leatherface, Mama, Tinker, Tex, Alfredo, and the little girl are far more reserved, more tactical, and perhaps even a little more sophisticated. Is it the presence of a woman that helps subdue Leatherface and the boys? Maybe her love and care gave him the confidence he clearly lacked in the first two films, under the scornful eye of an emotionally abusive older brother?

Something else has changed, though, as it's revealed that Ryan will provide more than enough meat and there will be no need to kill Michelle right away. They tell Leatherface he'll get to have some fun with her for a while and then comes the worst part. Mama tells Michelle that Leatherface makes the prettiest babies and there are hints that the little girl may be his daughter from some previous victim. Leatherface eyes Michelle calmly at this news. This is a far cry from the Leatherface we saw in *Part II*, as sexually confused as he was frustrated. Stretch had tricked him into believing he had sexually satisfied her with his chainsaw, and he let her live, clearly smitten with her. Later, when he discovers that she has followed him and Chop Top back to their hideout, he tries to make her his girlfriend, while at the same time treating her like a stray pet he's trying to sneak into the house. To me, this gives Leatherface a whole new level of danger and makes this is the most disturbing part of the film. Tex and Tinker are far more capable and level-headed than their previous counterparts. Tinker, true to his name, is an inventor of sorts and Tex is as handsome and charming as he is cruelly violent. The pair are never shrill or out of control. They go about the business of murder as two men getting ready to harvest a garden or slaughter a pig. While they wait for Leatherface to appear with Benny, Tinker brings out a massive, shiny, chrome-plated chainsaw, a gift to their brother. Earlier, we'd already seen Leatherface with a Walkman in his work shed and now this extravagant gift might be some insight into Leatherface's evolution and maturity. This new family dynamic uses positive re-enforcement to bring the stunted man-child into his own.

`

There's not much to Michelle and Ryan, at first. It's not until Benny tracks them back to the house and starts shooting up the place, giving Michelle a chance to escape (watching her pull her hands free from the nails is brutally awesome). Once Michelle is on her feet, she becomes a storm of rage, taunting Leatherface to chase her into the woods. With a bloody face and wild eyes, she screams at him, "You sick...fucker!" She's bordering on insanity herself, but she's not backing down and she's more than ready to fight. Kate Hodge shines at this point — she seriously becomes exciting to watch, not to say there was anything wrong with her performance overall, but at this point she's in the zone. There's a tense moment in the chase where she becomes snared in one of the family's booby traps as Leatherface closes in. She's rescued by Benny who seemingly gets taken out by Leatherface, who then quickly returns his attention to Michelle and gets his head smashed in for his trouble with a big rock.

I think it's fair to say *Leatherface* is far better than it deserves to be. Director Jeff Burr was brought on after Peter Jackson passed on the project and he had an incredibly tight shooting schedule (although I don't think it was nearly as tight as Hooper had on the previous instalment). In addition, Schow's script was gory, and the film had to be submitted to the MPAA 11 times to avoid an X rating (after Leatherface, the NC-17 rating was invented as a more appropriate rating). The result was a nearly bloodless Chainsaw film with none of the gore Part II had. While the R rating keeps the story intact, it's easy to feel cheated knowing that a chunk of the film wound up on the cutting room floor. Burr was unhappy with the finished product and wanted his name removed from the film, but it was too late as the prints were already produced. Though it made a decent profit, it's the third lowest rated film in the series, beating out *The Next Generation* and *Texas Chainsaw 3D* (2013).

North Star Comics, who published the original few issues of David Quinn and Tim Vigil's *Faust: Love of The Damned*, as well as work from James O'Barr (*The Crow*) and Kelley Jones (*Batman*), published a three-issue adaptation of the film based on Schow's uncut script. An unrated DVD is out there, and Warner Bros. Archives released a Blu-Ray release and it's also uncut.

1991

Following the release of the "most controversial horror film ever," Northstar Comics got the rights to do an adaptation of Schow's original screenplay. The adaptation was written by Bram Stoker Award winning horror author Mort Castle with art duties on issue one handled by Kirk Jarvinen and the last three issues drawn by Guy Burwell.

Northstar was the original home of David Quinn and Tim Vigil's *Faust: Love of the Damned*, a brutal, black and white comic series, full of graphic violence and pornographic sex. They also published work by *The Crow's* James O'Barr and by Schow, among others. So, there couldn't have been a better home for a *TCM* comic.

Castle wasn't confined to write a straight adaptation of Schow's script and was allowed to make some creative choices throughout the four issues, including tweaking some characters' fates and how the story ended. Any changes were ultimately inconsequential. The writing itself was solid, the artwork was fine, if uneven and at times amateurish. Dave Dorman (*Deadworld, Star Wars*) painted the cover for issue one, which makes it worth it for collectors alone.

Leatherface returned to comics in a four issue limited series from Topps Comics, where he befriended and then battled Jason Vorhees. Written by the great Nancy A Collins

(*Sunglasses After Dark, Swamp Thing*), penciled by Jeff Butler, with covers by Simon Bisley.

Much like the later film and comics with Freddy Krueger fighting Jason, the story takes place outside of the canon timelines of either character. Jason, following the events of *Jason Takes Manhattan*, wakes on a train, being mistakenly transported to Mexico to be dumped with the radioactive waste he was scooped up with. The train is derailed though, once Jason revives and starts murdering everyone. The train crashes in Texas, where Jason is found by Leatherface, who recognizes Jason as a kindred spirit and takes him home to the family. It's a story that makes more sense for *TCM*, not so much for *F13*, because Jason has never previously expressed patience for any humans.

Jason vs Leatherface was far less gruesome than the Schow/Castle Northstar series, but it did have the weird horror and humor that made Collins' run on *Swamp Thing* so interesting.

Unfortunately, both series are prohibitively expensive on the secondary market, especially *JvL*. And with the rights to these properties either moving around a lot or held up in court, who knows if they'll ever be reprinted.

(Sidenote, Topps also published a three-issue adaptation of *Jason Goes to Hell*, all of these came out while New Line Cinema held the rights to both franchises.)

1995

The original TCM quadrology of films came to a train wreck of a crashing halt in 1995 when Kim Henkel returned to direct *Texas Chainsaw Massacre Part 4* aka *Texas Chainsaw the Next Generation*. Henkel approached the film with some interesting ideas, but the execution is...lacking, to say the least. From the awful cast to the wasted cameos of original *TCM* alum, to the directionless script of recycled ideas, to the slap dash editing, *The Next Generation* is nothing but a punishing watch. When it came out in 95, it was promptly shelved, but two years later, to cash in on the rising stars of Renee Zellweger and Mathew McConaughey, it hit video store shelves.

At some point I had read an interview with Henkel, and I'm going to assume it was in *Fangoria*, where he talked about exploring Leatherface's sexuality or transsexuality which was hinted at in the original film, when Leatherface donned his "pretty lady" mask, but that didn't really come through. There was no exploration, just Leatherface going from dressing like a redneck to getting gussied up in lady face and torso and a black dress, which was just comically stupid and addressed nothing. The new family is just an inept group of disparate weirdos with no chemistry, yelling and being annoying, and McConaughey is the worst of the lot, at one point even doing an impression of a Tusken Raider(??). I do wonder if he was just spit-balling an unhinged routine, playing around in front of a camera/on set, to see what worked. Probably thinking that this piece of shit would never see the light of day. McConaughey is a fine actor, sometimes easy to laugh at, but when he's in the zone, he's absolutely fucking compelling-*True Detective* and *Killer Joe* immediately come to mind. Zellweger, for her part, is almost charming at times, and maybe if this were a straight parody of a *TCM* film she would have been a better fit?

    I swear, I've watched this movie five or six times and I just keep walking away wondering why the fuck I just can't accept that it really is as bad as it is. From the start, *The Next Generation* does everything the other *TCM* movies do; we get a new group of victims and they run afoul of the Sawyer clan. We get night chases, we get a dinner scene, we get chaos, but here it is never fun, never entertaining, never scary. The only time it does something interesting, is when a fucking limo pulls up and the fucking Illuminati comes in to critique the Sawyers' handling of this group of victims. That's right, the government, the 'deep state,' knows about and sanctions the Sawyer family for their own sick entertainment. Even this inspired bit of originality is never capitalized on, because we get...a RV driven by an old couple out of nowhere, a pointless chase scene, and a Deus ex machina crop duster swooping down and hitting Leatherface so Zellweger can escape...It's a mess, and this is the recut version from 97, released commercially!

Yes, this film has its fans and defenders, and yes, I'm speaking in broad strokes here, glossing over a lot of details, but I don't believe this film has an ounce of merit. There's no meat on the bone! And the Illuminati sub-plot, watch *True Detective* season one if you want to see the best possible version of this scenario. I don't know why Henkel would turn his greatest creation (talking about the original film, here) into a confusing and confused farce and then make a dig, in the opening crawl, at the previous two sequels as "unrelated, minor events." I have so much love for the first three films and see them as vital entries into the horror genre, so this has always pissed me off. Unfortunately, we would see this level of self-parody affect *Friday the 13th*, with *Jason X* and *Freddy's Dead* is certainly not the highlight of the *Nightmare on Elm Street* franchise, and don't get me started on *Halloween Resurrection*. It's no wonder we got a slew of remakes in the 2000s after all the original slasher franchises committed suicide with unwatchable sequels through the 90s.

2003

Speaking of-it was 2003 when *Texas Chainsaw Massacre* got its remake under Platinum Dunes, directed by Marcus Nispel and written by Scott Kosar. This film, along with its prequel, *TCM; The Beginning*, are fine films and well made. They're gory, the casts are decent to great, but I'll be damned if they just aren't saying anything to the point of being almost soulless. And maybe that's harsh, but as I've said, the original film was pure savage American art, these two films are slick and commercial. They don't feel dangerous, they're mere entertainment. And there's nothing wrong with entertainment or art for art's sake. Not everything has to have a message or really be about anything, but *TCM* 03 suffers for not...suffering. There's no desperation present in the performances of the cast and hell, Leatherface's mask doesn't even look homemade. It looks like it was designed by professional FX artists and it's that slickness that throws up a wall to having a visceral connection to the work. I do think *The Beginning* fares a little better, likely since David Schow co-wrote the script.

But what the 03 film got right, was the geek show aspect. The film is gorgeous to look at, shot by the original film's cinematographer, Daniel Pearl. The main protagonists are all very pretty and easy on the eyes, without a Franklin to cause any discomfort. Jessica Biel spends the runtime of the film with a bare midriff and tight pants. R Lee Ermey delivers the creepiest and most entertaining dialogue of the film, the way he did in *Full Metal Jacket*. The gore and violence don't hold back, and the film comes gleefully roaring to life with a graphic suicide then an amazing camera movement through the hole in the dead girl's head. The Sawyer clan is expertly grimy in the most cinematically pleasing way. It's all surface, though. It says nothing relevant about 2003 and doesn't mean anymore twenty years later.

This seems like a major missed opportunity, considering it was in production a year or so after 9/11. It may have been set in the same timeframe as the original, but with America swiftly moving into war right after suffering a traumatizing terrorist event that played out on live TV, and the peace and security Americans had taken for granted was suddenly shattered, it seems to me that *TCM* 03 was well positioned to be more than just a remake. It could have, should have, had something to say. Yes, you could argue that parts 3 and 4 weren't exactly brimming with social commentary, but the 90s weren't as tumultuous a decade as the two that bookend it. George Bush ended the 80s by driving us into a recession and a conflict with Iraq and his son, George W Bush, spent the early 2000s driving us back into a recession and another conflict in

Iraq. By contrast, Bill Clinton's 90s lacked any major tragedies, unjust military misadventures, or financial disasters. The social issues of the 90s were of a more sensitive nature-like for-profit prisons, gay rights, and the trans issues that Henkel wanted to explore in 4. I don't know why we really didn't get many deeper horror films, other than say, *Candyman* or *Nightbreed,* which I think is impossible to not read as a queer parable. Like it or not, horror was, is, and forever shall be political. Mindless, mean-spirited, and pointless movies abound, and are often a lot of fun, but the best of horror cinema is fueled by passion about an ideal; Romero's *Dead* films, Larry Fessenden's *The Last Winter,* Cronenberg's body of work, John Carpenter's *They Live.* The original *TCM* was a shout into the void during a dark period for America, so I believe the makers of 2003's unnecessary but entertaining remake owed it to Hooper and Henkel to put a little more substance into their pretty movie.

The Beginning, directed by Jonathan Liebesman (*Teenage Mutant Ninja Turtles*) and starring Jordanna Brewster and Matt Bomer, was unhampered by any such responsibility. A prequel to a remake isn't a place where I'm looking for a lot of thought, but weirdly, I found this movie overall more watchable than 03. It's a grittier and more transgressive rehash of the remake showing how Ermey became the sheriff and the family started eating people. Its utterly charmless and ugly, but there's a lot more fun to be had in that. Maybe I'm being unfair to 03, but that has nothing to do with it being a remake. I've been a defender of Rob Zombie's *Halloweens* and Platinum Dunes' *Friday the 13th* was a largely successful and, in many ways, better movie than the original three *F13s*. 03 should have tried harder.

Beginning brings nothing new to the table, but simply by using the aesthetic of torture porn with perhaps a bit of stolen audacity from New French Extremity, it wound up being a punchier entry that didn't need to do a lot of leg work.

2005

New Line Cinema re-licensed the *TCM* comic books in 2005, this time to Avatar Press, which became the home of the later issues of *Faust: Love of the Damned* and its handful of spin offs, as well books by Alan Moore, Warren Ellis, Joe R Lansdale, and an adaptation of Frank Miller's original *Robocop 2* screenplay. Maybe one the most notable and popular of Avatar's publications though, is the horrifically graphic *Crossed*. So, like Northstar, Avatar was an ideal home for *TCM* comics. Despite artwork by the great Jacen Burrows and Daniel HDR and scripts by *Lady Death* creator Brian Pulido, I could never engage with the mini-series and one shots that Avatar produced, because their output served as prequels and sequels to the Platinum Dunes films.

My overall disappointment is purely subjective. The creative teams that worked on these books are capable craftsmen, whose work I've enjoyed on other titles. So, for fans of the 03 and 05 remakes, these series are gold, deepening and expanding the storyline, further exploring the motivations of the family, and most importantly, going further with the sex and violence than the films were allowed to.

The first release was a one shot by Pulido and Burrows, simply called *Texas Chainsaw Massacre Special*, this was followed by a three-issue mini-series called *Texas Chainsaw*

`

Massacre: The Grind. The final release was *Texas Chainsaw Massacre: Fearbook* by Antony Johnston and Daniel HDR. That was the end of the line for Avatar though.

In 2007, New Line moved *Texas Chainsaw, Friday the 13th, and A Nightmare on Elm Street* to DC Comics' imprint Wildstorm. Wildstorm took a slightly different approach than Avatar by releasing a direct sequel to the 03 remake. Dan Abnett and Andy Lanning wrote the six-issue run while Wesley Craig handled the art duties. This set up a continuing story line which found Erin in a mental institution and Leatherface still on the loose, minus an arm.

Bruce Jones and Chris Gugliotti closed out Wildstorm's run with *Texas Chainsaw Massacre: Raising Cain*, introducing a set of twins for the Hewitts, named...Cain and Abel. Which isn't all that interesting, compared to Nubbins and Chop Top. The story was fine, but like everything else related to the 03 remake, it simply lacked the black comedic absurdity that made the two Hooper films so original and endearing.

To date, this was the last time *TCM* appeared in comics

2013

Millennium Films got the rights to *TCM* next, and in 2013 released Texas Chainsaw 3D. Though it was written by *Jason Goes to Hell's* Adam Marcus and Debra Sullivan, the movie was practically dead-on arrival as a direct sequel to the original film, ignoring all the other entries. Cameos by Bill Mosely, Gunnar Hansen, and Marilyn Burns, aside the film trips over its own dick almost immediately after a strong opening scene set in 1974, when we time jump to 2013 to find Alexandra Daddario's character, in her twenties, receiving a letter of inheritance from her real family that she's never heard of. Long story short, she's a Sawyer. Why is this a problem? Because we see her character as a baby in 1974 and now four decades later that baby is only in her early 20s! In Marcus and Sullivan's defense, their script was set in the 90s. The producers didn't want to do a period piece, but then didn't adjust for the time difference and shot and released the whole fucking movie like that. It's such a glaringly stupid thing, that it's hard to see all the good the film has going for it. It's an interesting premise, to have Daddario's character not only inheriting her grandmother's house, but that she also must become the caretake of Leatherface, who lives in the basement like a shameful family secret. There's a great backwoods family feud set up between the

Sawyers and the Hartman's who led a lynch mob that murders (most of) the Sawyers at the beginning of the film. And by the end of the film Daddario finds herself in an *Of Mice and Men* situation with Leatherface, which would have made a very compelling sequel. We didn't get a sequel though, did we? No, we got another prequel, this time to the original film, but through the retcon of the Millennium version.

Texas Chainsaw 3D really is the best Chainsaw we had gotten since *TCM III*. It does the smart thing of building out the world, showing the trauma caused by the Sawyer's actions, and exploring the dark secrets bubbling under the surface of a small town. We still get kids in a van on a road trip (Daddario as Heather, Tania Raymonde as Nikki, and Trey Songz as Ryan), they pick up a hitchhiker, and we think we know where this is going, but Marcus and Sullivan's script subverts our expectations, and when we finally meet Leatherface, he looks fantastically fucked up. Dan Yeager gives a solid performance as Leatherface, certainly channeling Mihailoff from *III* and he did such a great job it's a crime that there wasn't a sequel for him to come back for. As for the film's level of violence, it revels in the newfound freedom of the remakes with more splatter than previously allowed. KNB handled the effects, and it shows. The scene in Leatherface's workshop alone is worth showing up for. Leatherface has had problems in the past with victims running away, but he's learned from past failings and just cuts a guy in half. By the halfway point, director John Lussenhop sets a tone that would have made for a great trilogy of old man Leatherface films, had the movie not been savaged by fans and critics alike (the current IMDB ratings score is 4.8/10). But worldwide the film made back more than double its $20 million budget, in fact it made back its budget opening weekend. Not getting a sequel, based solely (seemingly, at least) on some surface level issues seems like a huge, missed opportunity.

The movie ends with some hanging threads that would have made for good story fodder, which is something *TCM* really never got, as opposed to the other big slasher franchises; *ANOES* had three films with Heather Langenkamp's Nancy and three films (3-5) that fed into each other, *F13* had the Tommy trilogy (4-6), and *Halloween* has had two Laurie trilogies (1,2, and *H20*, and 2018, *Kills,* and *Ends*) and the Jamie/Thorn trilogy (4-6). Meanwhile, *Scream* wisely continued focusing on Sidney Prescott for five films. The first three *TCMs* are the only ones that come close to a continuing narrative, but even with Hooper at the helm for the first two, it's still tenuous at best. Yes, the antagonist remains constant with all these franchises (with Ghostface it's a matter of semantics, because it's always a Ghostface costume regardless of who's underneath), but the best entries, or at least the fan favorites, all have a reoccurring protagonist. Without Laurie, Jamie, Tommy, Nancy, or Sydney you really are left with a geek show of fresh-faced nobodies lined up to die and if they're not coming back for the sequel, what is there to emotionally latch on to for fans? This is a completely subjective argument, of course. Some come to a slasher for the cool kills, and they don't care who the teens are. That's fine. Engage with art as you see fit, but for me, *A Nightmare on Elm Street* should have always been about Nancy. I love the franchise, but by *Freddy's Dead*, it was merely self-parody and a cynical cash grab. The Jamie/Thorn trilogy was an organic growth from part two with Jamie being Laurie's orphaned daughter and running from her uncle Michael, but when *H20* deep sixed that story and restarted from the end of part 2, it created a duo of cynical cash grabs of poor quality and no soul. Nowhere to go but do a remake.

So, we go back to my issues with the 03 remake of *TCM* and its prequel. It's an anti-throughline with nothing to say. *TCM* could function just fine focusing on the Sawyers, because it was about America and class, but imagine how much cooler *TCM III* would have been if Michelle and Ryan had been saved by Stretch instead of Benny? Hopper's Lefty, being the uncle to Sally and Franklin, already created the emotional bridge between 74 and 86. Stretch could have continued that into 93, maybe even

95. My theory has always been as to why these franchises have a hard time maintaining fan interest is that are too many people bringing new ideas without much regard for what came before, and not giving proper care to a cohesive narrative. Compare that to *Phantasm*, a five-film series that mostly kept the same stars across all the films and kept writer/director Don Coscarelli in control. Or *Evil Dead*, three films and three seasons of a TV series, under Sam Raimi, Robert Tappert, and Bruce Campbell's control. The through line and quality remains consistent and establishes them as two of the strongest horror franchises ever created. The slasher franchises are mostly helmed by a bunch of hired guns who may or may not even like these films that came before.

Digging out of this digression, Daddario's Heather becoming the caretaker of Leatherface while surviving members of the Hartman family and their allies come for them could have made for two more good films, but Millennium apparently got cold feet and ran with the safest option possible, another prequel.

2015

The long running, taboo busting action horror fighting game, *Mortal Kombat* added to its already cluttered cast of characters with *Mortal Kombat X*, a game I was excited as hell to get as the DLCs added the Predator, a xenomorph from *Alien*, Jason Vorhees, and Leatherface. The game's previous chapter had included Freddy Kreuger, and the following chapter added Rambo, Spawn, and the Terminator. I hadn't thought much about *Mortal Kombat* since I used to play the original game at the arcade, but nothing's going to get my attention faster than an opportunity to play as both Jason and Leatherface and make them fight to the death. Which was the very first thing my son and I did when we got home from the game shop.

Leatherface's movements were well developed, employing a synthesis of the variations of the character from the first movie and the remake. You can choose from three different skins; the "pretty lady" which is Leatherface's look from the climax of the 74 film, the "killer" which is supposed to be pulled from the 74 film as well but looks more like a mix of 74 and 03, and finally the "butcher' which comes from the 03 remake.

The only drawback to playing Leatherface (or Jason or any character in the game) is you're limited to the narrow parameters of the game. Leatherface is just a temporary guest and there's only so much mileage to gain from having him chainsaw through your favorite *MK* characters. Fighting games can never hold my attention for very long, because I like a slower paced, open world, story line, like the *Batman Arkham* games from Rocksteady or the *Call of Cthulhu* game from Cyanide. Still though, I can't knock *MKX* for any quality issues. The graphics are fantastic, the gore is cringeworthy, and though it got old for me, it was fun as hell for a significant stretch of time.

In 2017, Jason got his first solo video game since 1989, from Gun Media. *Friday the 13th the Game* was a crowd funded survival horror online game where you could either play as a camp counsellor with a group, trying to outwit and outrun Jason, or play as Jason in a series of missions, taking place at various famous *F13* locations, with a wide variety of skins to choose from and unlock, including a Tom Savini original design called Hell Jason.

Unfortunately, the pissing contest between director Sean Cunningham and writer Victor Miller over the rights to *F13* that has resulted in a multi-year legal battle killed the game, ending all possibilities of updates and add-ons. All was not lost though, as Gun announced their next project would be the *Texas Chainsaw Massacre.*

The game would function in much the same way as *F13*, but instead of your group trying to survive one killer, you'll need to survive the whole Sawyer clan at various maps based on film locations. The game launches in 2023, but

Gun has only released a teaser trailer and some gameplay footage as of this writing.

Leatherface was also added as a DLC for the slasher/survival game *Dead by Daylight*, along with Freddy, Ghostface, and Pinhead. You play as Leatherface stalking and slashing victims with far more latitude than you could ever get with *Mortal Kombat*. Similarly, a Leatherface DLC was added to *Call of Duty: Modern Warfare*. That was never a franchise I was interested in playing and not even the inclusion of Bubba was going to get me dropping money on it. I hear it was a fairly successful collaboration and I'm glad everyone had fun.

2017

2017's Leatherface is my favorite *TCM* film since part 3. Written by Seth Sherwood and directed by New French Extremity duo Julien Maury and Alexandre Baustillo (*Inside*) and starring Stephen Dorff and Lili Taylor. The film is set in the 1950s and we see Leatherface as a boy being ripped from his family and growing up in an asylum and then as a teenager escaping with a dangerous group of violent psychopaths, with a nurse as a hostage. *Leatherface* is a Jim Thompson-esque Splatterpunk road movie, full of real nastiness. Artfully directed with some strong performances from the whole cast and only hurt by the single conceit of us not knowing which of these psychos will turn into Leatherface. It's a silly and pointless element, with some obvious misdirection, but for me, it didn't hurt my overall enjoyment of the film. *Leatherface* is truly the fiercest entry into the franchise since Burr's *Leatherface*, but this time Maury and Baustillo were unhampered by the need to cut the film down for an R rating.

What hurts *Leatherface* more than anything is being the second prequel in a franchise that also has three part 2s. All this says is, the various studios really don't know what to do with *TCM* as a series, because the first film was so singular and never *needed* a sequel or prequel.

So, it's too bad that one of the franchise's finest moments arrives in as seemingly a disposable entry as conceivable. Maury and Baustillo create a world that from the start is far less unhinged and doomed than most of the other films but does a great job of spinning reality out of control, so that by the end we can see the world of Hooper's original emerging.

The writing/directing duo had announced themselves as a force with *A L'Interieur* (*Inside*), part of the wave of New French Extremity, which included Alexandre Aja's *Haute Tension* and Pascal Laughier's *Martyrs*, among many others. New French Extremity is a self-explanatory phrase and a film movement that challenged the very notion of where the boundaries of horror really laid. The violence and sexuality, taboo busting set pieces, and politically thought-provoking idealism set films like *Frontier(s)* apart from your average American slasher, even putting Italian gore films to shame with how emotionally distressful many of the films are.

If the franchise needed anything, it was a visionary creative team to, not re-invent the wheel, just put new tires on the damn car. At first glance it may look like Millennium just tossed out another seemingly disconnected entry into a seemingly disconnected franchise, but it truly is a prequel to not just the original *TCM*, but their own *3D*. Dorf's character is a Hartman, so we're establishing the family feud going all the way back to the 50s at least. Lily

Taylor's Verna is Heather's (Daddario) grandmother who entrusted Leatherface's care to her. We see a young Drayton and Nubbins (but no Chop Top, which I wag my finger at), and we see how Leatherface could exist between two worlds, one of abject poverty and desperation, and one of wealth, as we see in *3D*.

I liked *Leatherface* from the first viewing, but subsequent watches and research made me appreciate it all the more. After the critical back hand *3D* got, Millennium would have been justified in scrapping what they started trying to build, and a prequel looks like the exact type of cynical 'fuck it' one would expect, but Maury and Baustillo saw what worked in the timeline and was impressed by Sherwood's excellent script and delivered a bad ass prison break/road movie. You can feel the Jim Thompson and Sam Peckinpah in the DNA *Leatherface*, almost as if the creative team had taken personal offense to Steve McQueen demanding Thompson's real ending to *The Getaway* be axed for something more Hollywood, and they stretched that madness out for a whole movie and liberally hosed it down with their own mad aesthetics.

Also, like *3D*, *Leatherface* breaks the repeated cycle of the first six movies where hapless victims dummy into the Sawyer (or Hewitt) house and get eaten. *3D* subverts the expectations, while *Leatherface* tosses it out the window. We turn back the clock to the 1950's, finding Betty Hartman (daughter of Dorf's Hal Hartman) and Ted Hardesty (future father of Sally and Franklin Hardesty) on a date, driving down a country road, when they come across a young Leatherface, Jedidiah (which was also the name he went by in *3D*, as opposed to Bubba in part 2), who appears to be injured. We know this is merely a trap, but Betty follows the boy on to a farm and into a barn, where she's seized upon by Drayton, Nubbins, and Jed. They brutalize and murder Betty. Later, her father, Sheriff Hal Hartman arrives on the scene, knowing it can only be the Sawyers behind this, he seizes Jed, and brings him to the Gorman House Youth Reformatory.

There's a ten-year time jump, and we learn that Verna has married a man with money and was able to get a court order finally giving her visitation rights to see her son. But Doctor Lang (Christopher Adamson) blocks her, despite the court order, so Verna instigates a riot, leading to a massacre of staff and patients alike, but gives a window for Jackson (Sam Strike) to escape, while protecting a nurse, Lizzy (Vanessa Grasse), who was kind to him and his friend Bud (Sam Coleman), who escapes with them. Unfortunately, Ike and Clarice (James Bloor and Jessica Madsen), two bat shit crazy patients as in love with violence as with each other, joins them, and Lizzy becomes a hostage, as they tear ass across Texas. We're led to believe that one of the three boys is Jedidiah, whose identity was masked by the state. The hulking silent Bud is far too obvious, Ike is almost definitely out from the moment we meet him, leaving the sensitive Jackson as the clear choice. There was an earlier idea to also make Clarice a possible candidate for the skin mask, but it was dropped pre-production. As I said, this is the only part of the story I didn't like. The twist was obvious, leaving out the mystery wouldn't have hurt the overall narrative. It would have been better to criss-cross more with the weird dynamics of the family as they scrambled to prepare for Jed's big homecoming. Seeing Dorf become increasingly unhinged in his pursuit to kill Jed is some of the actor's best work, in my opinion. Dorf and Taylor's performances add a lot of valuable strength to the production. Taylor wasn't the first choice to play Verna, though, she replaced Angela Bettis (*May, The Woman, Toolbox Murders*) who had to drop out due to scheduling conflicts.

For his part, screenwriter Sam Sherwood went to great lengths to pay respectful tribute to the first three films, while crafting a story that when viewed in chronological order could be understood and enjoyed by new viewers, creating a non-convoluted throughline from *Leatherface*, to *TCM 74*, to *3D*, but left room for fans to plug in 2 and 3 if they wanted. He did do a series of rewrites at the request of Maury and Baustillo, who wanted many aspects changed or toned down, including a thirty-person massacre at the end. I would have liked to have seen what Sherwood came up with for a follow up to *3D*, but because of delays getting *Leatherface* out Millennium lost the rights to the series, which was acquired by Legendary.

2022

As I'm writing this in October of 2022, I'm still reeling over how great of a year this has been for horror. On top of a slew of new, original releases, we've seen the third part of the new *Halloween* trilogy, *Halloween* Ends, an all-new *Hellraiser*, that has successfully restored the franchise to its former majesty, an all-new Dario Argento giallo, *Dark Glasses*, a better *Predator* than we've seen since part 2, *Prey*, a new *Scream*, Ti West launched a new slasher trilogy with *X* and *Pearl*, an unrated *Terrifier 2* getting a wide release, and most relevantly, the new *Texas Chainsaw* Massacre.

The rights to *Texas Chainsaw Massacre* have, as of now, been purchased by Legendary, home of the recent Godzilla movies, with Fede Alverez serving as producer and David Blue Garcia in the director's chair. Garcia replaced Ryan and Andy Tohill, who were fired after production was underway because the studio was unhappy with their results. Chris Thomas Devlin got the job as screenwriter, developing the script based off the original story written by Alvarez and Rodo Sayagues. Despite a rocky start, Alvarez and Garcia had a sturdy cast and a good script.

There was news that this would be another part 2, continuing a trend of simply reusing the original film's title, and serving as a "requel" or a redo sequel, once again ignoring every film but the original, like *Halloween 2018*. Alvarez later clarified that the original sequels were still part of the timeline, but I'm assuming he's only talking about the first two or first three. Exactly what happened to Leatherface in the ensuing decades is left largely ambiguous and up to interpretation or fan theory. But with news that the film would go straight to Netflix, many fans started having doubts that this would be the *TCM* film to bring the franchise 'back.'

Despite the sheer unkindness of critics and many fans, *TCM 2022* held the #1 spot on Netflix for a couple of weeks.

We open with a group of young people, who we learn are influencers, on their way to a small, out of the way town, to meet with investors about buying up the town and turning it into a bit of bourgeois utopia, separate from the violence and crime of the big city, specifically after Melody's (Sarah Yarkin) younger sister Lila (Elsie Fisher) survived a school shooting. Class and elitism play into this narrative quickly, as the young people, including Dante (Jacob Lattimore) and Ruth (Nell Hudson) have a run in with a local hick named Richter (Moe Dunford) and local law enforcement. At every turn through the opening moments, stock characters play against type and subvert stereotypes. The legendary Alice Krige from *Sleepwalkers* and *Psycho IV*, plays Ginny, who lives in and owns the orphanage that we learn has been Leatherface's home since (at least off and on) 1974. Leatherface is the last resident of the orphanage, which begs several questions, like does Ginny know who Leatherface really is? We see that he has hidden his chainsaw within the walls later in the film. It's hard to imagine Ginny would not have known about that. So, could she be a caretaker like Verna and Heather was in *3D*? Maybe another family member giving Leatherface shelter, like his families in 3 and *Next Generation*?

Mark Burnham dons the skin mask this time around, again channeling part 3's Mailhoff more than Gunnar Hansen's original portrayal. His Leatherface is a quiet, calm-before-the-storm. He's immobile and unmasked when we first get a glimpse of him, but he leaps into action, moving with a deftness, sure of his steps, when Ginny has an episode and needs to be rushed to the hospital.

This episode followed, not quite a misunderstanding, but a clash of cultures when the young people request that a Confederate flag be removed, and Ginny tries to assure Dante, an African American, that she doesn't keep it up because she's racist, its that it belonged to her great-great grandfather. Adding to her stress and ultimately causing her breakdown, is the realization that these young people are there to take her home. As she insists that she still owns the property she collapses and Leatherface bursts in to protect her.

`

We get a shade of Leatherface from *3D*, as he was Verna's caretaker there as much as she had been his. We don't get much of a sense of how Leatherface has been living or what he has been doing all these decades. If we can assume the first three films are still canon, then we can assume Leatherface has been behaving like a tom cat, occasionally wandering off and hooking up with various family members, and then making his way back to Ginny when things go awry. Has he been on the hunt for Ginny? Is Ginny also a cannibal? Its left up to interpretation. This film is more concerned with the story at hand, than building on too many aspects of the legacy. Any of that really falls on Sally Hardesty (Owlen Fouere) to carry.

There's no getting around the comparisons of 2022's Sally Hardesty and *Halloween* 2018's Laurie. Both older women, who have survived their trauma, and became gun-toting bad asses. The primary difference is that Sally has become a Texas Ranger (a nod to Lefty). So, when Sally comes to town shooting up the place with her shotgun, she's at least sanctioned to do so. Fouere is great in the role (the original Sally, Marylin Burns had passed away years earlier after filming a small cameo in *3D*, playing Verna) and is as much a highlight to this film as she was in *Mandy*. Sally's role isn't huge, and the movie doesn't hinge on her as much as it exploits that first film connection, but I think her sudden appearance and capabilities serve as an inspiration to Lila and Melody to not give up and keep fighting, regardless of their age and gender, and it was certainly a passing of the torch, and I sincerely hope we see Lila and Leatherface face off again.

One thing that's been stuck in my craw since the film debuted, is this nonsense about *TCM2022* being the "woke" Chainsaw film. Children, sit down while the adults are talking. There is nothing "woke" about this movie. There is a clash of cultures, but at every turn, stock characters play against stereotype, do or say something unexpected, and evolve over the course of the movie. The main cast is actually well written and well rounded, with the stock secondary characters existing for body count and comic relief. It works. All art being subjective, not liking the movie for a myriad of reasons is valid, but not liking this one because it is "woke" shows you didn't watch it or didn't pay attention. It's not a deep movie, it has no agenda to hide. The filmmakers embraced the franchise with love and respect, crafted a modern, accessible storyline, and delivered a fun, fast paced, and gory sequel. The fact that there are modern kids in this movie is why some are calling it "woke" the same way any movie made by a non-white/non-male "has an agenda." That's projection.

As I'm writing this, we're only two years away from the original *Texas Chainsaw Massacre* turning fifty years old. Leatherface has joined the ranks of Dracula and Frankenstein as a classic movie monster. He's conquered the worlds of cinema, comics, games, and toys. We just need a *TCM* novel or two (his slasher contemporaries, Jason, Freddy, and Michael have all appeared in literature in the 1980s and 90s, but Leatherface only appeared in one novelization for the 03 remake, adapted by Stephen Hand).

With Gun Media's game on the way and the success of the 2022 Netflix movie guaranteeing another film, the future looks good for *Texas Chainsaw Massacre*. Tobe Hooper, Kim Henkel, Kit Carson, David Schow, and Jeff Burr all had an essential hand in inspiring me as a storyteller and still do to this day. The 1974 original still stands tall as a shocking and disturbing cinematic journey into a true heart of darkness. The quality of the sequels may be unequal, but aside from *The Next Generation*, they're never less than entertaining.

PRECURSORS, RELATIVES, AND KNOCK OFFS

A grim real-life coincidence is the true crime scene known as the Texas Killing Fields, outside League City, Texas not far from Houston. Thirty-three bodies have been dumped there, with many more women disappearing from the area over the years. It's believed to be a dumping ground for multiple serial killers. A twenty-five acre stretch of hell off I-45, The Killing Fields have been the subject of a feature film, 2011's *The Texas Killing Fields*, and a documentary, Netflix's 2022 *Crime Scene: The Texas Killing Fields*. *The Nowhere Dispatch*, a podcast dedicated to the weird history and happenings of East Texas also had a chilling episode dedicated to the Fields. I don't want to be exploitative drawing comparisons between a work of fiction and true-life horror, but I've always found the co-existence of the two chilling. The opening of *Leatherface: The Texas Chainsaw Massacre Part III* starts with the discovery of one of the Sawyer's body dumps and it's the scariest part of the film. I've never found anyone connected to the films' claim any inspiration from the crimes, but I think Ranger Lefty's pursuit, going crime scene to crime scene could have been a subconscious nod, at least.

`

The more famous real-life crime is that of Ed Gein, obviously. Gein has launched plenty of works of horror fiction, *Psycho* and *TCM,* being the most famous. Then there's Sawney Bean of the UK, an inbred clan that hid in caves in Scotland and was believed to have attacked and eaten a thousand people over twenty-five years before the whole 45-member clan was finally put to death (although, some historians question the factualness of this legend). That story had a clearer influence on Wes Craven's *The Hills Have Eyes* and Jack Ketchum's *Offseason, Offspring,* and *The Woman.*

Gein was a grave robber and decorated his house with body parts, make clothing from human skin, and even kept his mother's corpse in his farmhouse. Robert Bloch based *Psycho* on broad strokes of the case, without getting the full story before writing the novel. Alfred Hitchcock's 1960 adaptation made the Gein stand in, Norman Bates, far more sympathetic than Bloch did in the book, in fact the *Psycho* sequels in film vs literature are very different. Early in Bloch's *Psycho II*, Norman rapes a nun's corpse, meanwhile in Richard Franklin's *Psycho 2,* Norman is a sad victim.

Herschell Gordon Lewis had the first explicitly bloody cannibal flick out of the gate with his 1963 gore flick, *Blood Feast*. Then in 64 served up some ghostly killer redneck horror with *2000 Maniacs*. The geek show is on full display with Lewis's charming and silly features, but I think, considering Hooper was pursuing a PG rating for *TCM* that he wasn't trying to emulate Lewis's approach or embrace of gore for shock factor.

Jack Hill's 1967 obscure classic *Spider Baby* tells the story of a demented family that suffers from a very rare familial madness that turns them into cannibals. This movie should be far better known. Lon Chaney Jr plays the patriarch of the family, in one of his best and last roles. If you take *Spider Baby* and *TCM* you have the parents of Rob Zombie's *House of 1000 Corpses* (more on that later).

In 1972, Gary Sherman (*Poltergeist III*) made *Death Line*, aka *Raw Meat* with Christopher Lee and Donald Pleasence, beating Wes Craven to a modern-day retelling of the Sawney Bean legend, this time beneath the streets of London in unused sections of the tube. *Death Line* is a fantastic film with some great verbal sparring between Lee and Pleasance.

Alan Ormsby's (*Children Shouldn't Play with Dead Things*) *Deranged: Confessions of a Necrophile* was a docu-drama of the Gein case, that beat *Texas Chainsaw Massacre* to the big screen by several months (February 74 vs October 74). There's something so cheap and exploitative about the movie from the title to the movie poster and VHS/DVD cover art, but the film itself is a well-made, slow burn, and disturbing piece of filmmaking (the same can be said of *Children*). The only downside to the movie is the frequent interruptions from the crime reporter who just walks into scenes and starts monologuing. Ezra Cobb is the stand in Gein, played to perfection by Robert Blossoms. The movie really gets under your skin in places but compared to *TCM* it lacks the cultural sledgehammer to cement its place in popular culture. So, now it's just a footnote in horror history but deserves to be better known.

1973's *Malatesta's Carnival of Blood* is worth noting for being a weird and nasty slice of regional horror about a vampire who runs a carnival that serves as a buffet for cannibalistic ghouls who live beneath the carnival. It's another notable footnote that probably remains unknown to many horror fans. I'd never heard of it before it was included in Arrow Video's *American Horror Project Volume One*.

In 1976, Hooper released *Eaten Alive*, a twisted East Texas swamp movie, about a hotel owner that murders guests and feeds them to his pet alligator. With a cameo from Marilyn Burns and an early appearance by Freddy himself, Robert Englund, *Eaten Alive* is a deliriously twisted proto slasher that makes a worthy follow-up to *TCM*. Its far sleazier and more mean-spirited, though, and in a sense feels less accomplished than its predecessor. Maybe it's because of the budget, because over the next several years, Hooper would go on to make the modern classics *Salem's Lot*, *The*

Funhouse, and *Poltergeist* all of which display his powerful hold on the craft.

    Wes Craven followed up his gritty and disturbing 1972 debut, *Last House on the Left*, with 1977's *The Hills Have Eyes*. *Last House* was itself a foundational building block for modern horror, alongside George Romero's *Night of the Living Dead*. Add *TCM* and Bob Clark's *Black Christmas* and you have the four pillars of modern horror. Despite its place in history, *Last House* didn't propel Craven's career and it took him five years to get his next picture into production. Borrowing *TCM's* set designer, Robert Burns, Craven and crew headed out to the punishing and desolate desert to film his take on the Sawney Bean legend. Plot-wise, you could switch out Michael Berryman's Jupiter for Leatherface and we could've had *TCM2* nine years earlier. That's not to say Craven's film isn't fantastic and worthy of respect. I'm personally a big fan of it (not a fan *The Hills Have Eyes 2*, though, that is truly a slog). *Hills* follows a family taking a wrong turn and driving right into the hunting ground of an inbred family of cannibals. (I also highly recommend Alex Aja's fantastic remake, and its sequel is good as well.)

    David Schmoeller's 1979 *Tourist Trap* has the feel and some aesthetics in common with *TCM*, but instead of backwoods killers with a BBQ joint, you get a backwoods killer with a weird tourist attraction and telekinetic powers. It certainly exists because of *TCM* but

Schmoeller went off in his own weird direction, adding one of the more unique characters of the burgeoning slasher sub-genre in Chuck Connor's Slauson.

Kevin Connor's *Motel Hell*, from 1980, is a VHS classic, but for me it's just ok. Allegedly, there was a version of this film's script that was not a horror comedy but was a much more hardcore affair. For every great moment the film offers, it's dragged down by over acting, silly situations, and poor dialogue. The famous scene of Farmer Vincent wielding a chainsaw while wearing a pig head is about the most noteworthy thing in this film.

Also from 1980, Joe D'Amato's infamous *Anthropophagus* took the basic set up of *TCM*, moved it to a remote island off the coast of Greece, and gave us a graphic scene of a fetus being consumed as well as George Eastman's antagonist cannibal eating his own guts.

Juan Piquer Simon's 1982 *Pieces* deserves a nod for one of its two classic tag lines, "You don't have to go to Texas to have a chainsaw massacre." Otherwise, the movie has about as much of a connection to *TCM* as Bill Lustig's *Maniac*.

The real cannibal action was taking place in Italy around this time, though instead of backwoods rednecks it was indigenous cannibalistic tribes in South America. Umberto Lenzi's *Eaten Alive* and Ruggero Deodato's *Cannibal Holocaust*, along with *Man from Deep*

River, Cannibal Apocalypse, and *Cannibal Ferox* led a slew of knock offs that cannibalized the sub-genre out of existence. They're only worth mentioning regarding *TCM* as they all ran afoul of the British Board of Censors and branded Video Nasties. In fact, *TCM* was so hated, it tainted every movie with a power tool in the title, so *Driller Killer* was DOA in Britain.

In 1986, Michael Mann brought Thomas Harris's *Red Dragon* to the big screen as *Manhunter*, introducing the public at large to Hannibal the Cannibal, played by Brian Cox, though he was the secondary villain, behind Tom Noonan's Francis Dollarhyde aka The Tooth Fairy. But it was in Jonathan Demme's *Silence of the Lambs* where Hannibal became an academy award winning phenomenon. This time Anthony Hopkins stepped into the role of Hannibal as a more prominent but still secondary villain to Ted Levine's Buffalo Bill, a serial killer who skins women to make a pretty lady suit. They call this a "thriller," not a horror movie. Sure, Jan.

2003's *Wrong Turn* is a fairly blatant rip off of both *TCM* and *The Hills Have Eyes*, with mutant, inbred rednecks hunting and eating hapless idiots that dummy into their stretch of the woods. I liked the sequel directed by Joe Lynch and starring Henry Rollins, but I've never had any interest in continuing the series beyond that.

Andrew van den Houten adapted the Jack Ketchum novel, *The Offspring* in 2009, which is the sequel to Ketchum's notorious novel *Offseason*. To date that book has never been adapted for some reason. I've resisted seeing this film because I haven't read the book yet. I have seen 2011's *The Woman* from Lucky McKee, based on the book by Ketchum and McKee, not knowing it was the third part in a quadrology that includes Pollyanna McIntosh's *Darling*.

One of the most significant of the *TCM* inspired films must be Rob Zombie's 2003 *House of 1000 Corpses*. The White Zombie front man's debut film had a rocky start with the graphic content of the film making it hard to get distribution after Universal shelved it in 2000, believing it would receive a NC-17, the kiss of death for a theatrically released film. Zombie was able to get the rights and the film found a home with MGM briefly and finally settled at Lionsgate. Critical response was lukewarm, but the film enjoys a hardcore cult following, as does the superior sequel *The Devil's Rejects*, less so it seems the third part of the trilogy, *3 From Hell*. What sets *H1KC* apart from the other *TCM* knock offs is the deep reverence for grindhouse and drive-in exploitation Zombie has. It really comes through in the attention detail and the balls to the wall action and performances. It never feels as dangerous as *TCM*, though. For all it has going for it in art direction, cinematography, and grindhouse clout with Karen Black, Sid Haig, and Bill Moseley in front of the camera, it's hard to ignore the fact that it was shot on the Universal back lot, using the same house as Dolly Parton's *Best Little Whore House in Texas*. There's a slickness and a cartoonish vibe that makes it comparable to a kick ass episode of *Scooby Doo*, and I don't mean that disparagingly, I'm still a big fan.

The thing is though, *The Devil's Rejects* just works better in my eyes. Zombie is working with a smaller budget, shooting on location, and delivering a more realistic, scary, and insane experience the second time around and Moseley, Haig, and Sherri Moon Zombie get to flex their acting skills a lot more, delivering performances that swing between terrifying, absurd, and hilarious. Moseley in particular gets some of the best lines, like, "I am the Devil, and I am here to do the Devil's work," or "The next words out of your mouth had better be some brilliant Mark Twain shit, because it's definitely going on your tombstone."

Regarding both films, I feel like *TCM* is the secondary influence behind *Spider Baby*, which also starred a young Sid Haig. But Sid's Captain Spaulding has a lot more in common with Drayton Sawyer aka "The Cook," as a serious entrepreneur that also fronts a family of crazies, cannibals, rapists, and murderers. And of course, the *TCM* connection is undeniable with Chop Top himself, Bill Moseley taking center stage for the whole trilogy as Otis B Driftwood. Otis is far more reserved in his mania than Chop Top, but Moseley's performances are chilling. The actor who seems so funny and charming in interviews becomes otherworldly evil at times, shining most brightly in *Rejects*. If there's a "Leatherface" in the Firefly clan, it would be Tiny, played by Mathew McGrory, who at 7 feet 6 inches held the record for being the tallest actor on film. He had a larger role in *House* but was barely seen in *Rejects*, though his small role was pivotal. He died in 2005.

    Keeping *TCM* in the cultural conversation certainly hasn't hinged on Zombie, but it didn't hurt either. After Zombie's *Halloween* remake many people, especially those who didn't like his rough and white trash take on Michael Meyers, asked, if he was going to remake a horror classic, why not *TCM*? And yea, on the surface, it seems like a better fit, except he's already been there and done it with *House* and it wouldn't matter anyway, because there's a legion of keyboard warriors set to hate everything he does anyway, sight unseen. As far as I'm concerned, *House* and *Rejects* scratched that *Chainsaw* itch I had between Jeff Burr and David Schow's *Part III* and Julien Maury and Alexandre Bustillo's *Leatherface*, those being the best and most watchable of all the *TCM's* after the original and part 2.

    My favorite of all *TCM* inspired films, though would be Jill Gevargizian's *The Stylist*.

Based on her 2016 short film, the 2020 feature follows a shy and disturbed hair stylist with a dark secret. I was blown away by the short, especially a gore effect scalping that featured a sound effect that was grosser than the visual. The feature has been compared to *Maniac,* and that's an apt comparison. The complicated portrayal of lead character Claire (played by Najarra Townsend) is a twisted, sad, and engrossing journey, making her hard to hate even as she does horrible things, much like Joe Spinell's portrayal of Frank Zito. Gevargizian, though cited *TCM* as her primary influence though.

"EVERYTHING I've made and done is inspired by *The Texas Chainsaw Massacre*." Jill posted on Facebook after the death of Tobe Hooper in 2017. "Rest in peace to the master: Tobe Hooper. I have the Chainsaw tattoo. I visited the house from the film. I met all the actors. I directed a performance art tribute to southern horror years before I became a filmmaker, where Michael Huck played Leatherface. *The Stylist* was my attempt at creating a female Leatherface."

I can see that, imagine Leatherface's daughter from Part III, being taken into custody, growing up in the system, put on meds, years of therapy, moved out of state, and growing up with hazy memories of what life once was, as she navigates adulthood alone, with strange needs and drives she can't control...totally tracks. But independent of the *TCM* influence, *The Stylist* is gorgeously shot, tension filled, and has incredible performances from Townsend and Brea Grant. The fact that the movie succeeds on its own steam with the *TCM* influence as subtext is one of the things that elevates it in mind, as well. No need for a mush mouth galoot, or backwoods setting, *The Stylist* approaches its characters in crisis, speaking to their own time and place without explicitly leaning on any particular trope.

  This list could go on, but those films are minor and not foundational. It takes more than a backwoods redneck to make a *TCM* comparison and besides, for all the imitators and precursors, *TCM* remains a singular work of savage American art, unequaled and indisputable.

HORROR IS MY LIFE

I've said many times that horror and punk rock saved my life. It's true. Growing up poor, bouncing around from low rent housing to trailers to cheap apartments and growing up in a redneck small town with nothing to do and nowhere to go made me feel desperate and I was constantly reaching for something to give me a direction, a purpose, and an identity. Horror movies were my punk rock before I'd even heard of the Sex Pistols. But I feel there's a strong connection between the two and why they remain at the forefront of various inspirations and why I always turn back to them.

As there were already plenty of punk rock forebearers prior to bands like Black Flag or Misfits, *Texas Chainsaw Massacre* didn't exist in a vacuum either. As I've broken down, the elements of the story weren't even original, but it was the way Tobe Hooper and Kim Henkle approached, understood, remixed, and presented their pieces of art and the extremes they were willing to go that set them apart from other horror filmmakers, including gorier and more extreme directors like Herschell Gordon Lewis and Wes Craven. It's like Hooper was able to lasso a tornado and tame it like Pecos Bill.

"Art should comfort the disturbed and disturb the comfortable," opined Cesar A Cruz.

Punk and horror are two of the greatest embodiments of this philosophy. But there's another philosophy at play here that *TCM* seems to address with its very existence; Thomas Hobbes wrote in *Leviathan* that life in a world with no sovereign government would be "solitary, poor, nasty, brutish, and short." For the Sawyers in the 1970s and punk bands in the 1980s, both living under failed Republican administrations (Nixon and Reagan, respectively), times were dire. If it wasn't Vietnam or the oil crisis, it was The Cold War and the looming threat of nuclear apocalypse. Desperation responds with desperation, whether that's eating people or screaming your guts out at a hostile audience. Extreme? Apocalyptic fiction is often accompanied by cannibalism; Brian Keene's *The Rising,* Cormac McCarthy's *The Road*, Robert Kirkman's *The Walking Dead.* Food, water, and gas are three things worth killing for and the Sawyers were isolated in a dead part of Texas where all three were scarce, of course the familial madness seemingly passed down from Grandpa plays a large part in their perception of their situation, but like poor people trapped in horrible situations around the world, simply relocating to places with food, water, and gas is nearly impossible due to finances and geography. And like Jello Biafra said, "if you teach people that life is cheap and leave them to rot in ghettos and jails, they may one day feel justified in coming to rob and kill you. Duh."

Punk bands like Black Flag, DOA, Circle Jerks, and X survived on the road, like the biker gang in *Dawn of the Dead*. Their desperation stemmed from being disparate misfits from varying backgrounds, linked by a hunger to be heard and literal hunger. The streets of Los Angeles were deadly in real life; filled with threats of physical violence, sexual assault, murder, gun violence, and drug addiction. I think Penelope Spheeris could have made *TCM* as *Suburbia* and it wouldn't have strayed too far into something absurd. Alice Cooper once remarked that his whole schtick was really a reflection of America. "The sicker you get, the sicker we'll get." That sentiment echoes through punk, metal, and the best horror movies, regardless of era.

I remember being in grade school believing that Russia was going to nuke us at any moment. That *The Road Warrior* was a glimpse into the future. Sometimes I wonder if embracing my doom so young is why horror and punk were so love at first sight for me. Now, we're two years out from another failed Republican administration (Trump), an economic crisis, an oil shortage, Russia threatening nukes, spikes in homelessness, food shortages, droughts, environmental collapse, and, oh, a pandemic. *The Texas Chainsaw Massacre* is a catharsis in the face of a seemingly impending doom. Horror now more than ever. It's a salve for a wounded heart and a fractured mind. If we're all going to be screaming into the void, we might as well look cool doing it, have a kick ass soundtrack, and make the best movies while we're at it.

-12.17.2022

Also Available from St Rooster Books

From Tim Murr

The Gray Man
978-1799252177

Lose This Skin; Collected Short Works 1994-2011

978-1530351633
Conspiracy of Birds/Hounds of Doom
978-1516920631
City Long Suffering
978-1519588074
Motel on Fire; Stories
978-1543039016
Neon Sabbath; Stories

978-1721039708
My Skull is Full of Black Smoke; Stories
979-8680276099

Collection/Various Authors
To Be One with You; An Anthology of Parasitic Horror 2018 featuring Paul Kane, Marie O'Regan, Jeffery X Martin, Peter Oliver Wonder, Adam Millard, DJ Tyrer, David W Barbee, Ross Peterson
978-1724516787
Kids of the Black Hole; A Punksploitation Anthology featuring Sarah Miner, Chris Hallock, Paul Lubaczewski, and Jeremy Lowe

978-1072962724

The Blind Dead Ride Out of Hell; A Literary Tribute to the Amando de Ossorio Films featuring Sam Richard, Heather Drain, Paul Lubaczewski, Mark Zirbel, Jeremy Lowe, and Jerome Reuter

979-8692365187

A New Life by Paul Lubaczewski

979-8615384066

Blood & Mud by John Baltisberger

The God Provides by Thomas R Clark

979-8520227076

3 Hits from the Holler by Paul Lubaczewski

979-8707581984

Abhorrent Siren by John Baltisberger

978-1955745024

Let the World Drown: An Anthology of Sea Horror featuring Brian M Sammons, Lee Franklin, Jedediah Smith, AK McCarthy, Anthony S Buoni, BE Goose, Paul Lubaczewski, Jeremy Lowe, John Baltisberger, and Carter Johnson

979-8739852915

Souls in a Blender by Lamont A Turner

979-8494735201

Hungry Cosmos by Reed Alexander

979-8776862472

Black Friday: An Elder's Keep Collection by Jeffery X Martin

978-1955745093

Abhorrent Faith by John Baltisberger

978-1955745093

Short Stories About You by Jeffery X Martin

9798438145318
I Never Eat...Cheesesteak by Paul Lubaczewski
979-8440821415
Hunting Witches by Jeffery X Martin
979-8832793955
Saint's Blood by Ryan C Bradley
979-8804031863
As the Night Devours Us by Villimey Mist
979-8834327097
Parham's Field by Jeffery X Martin
SummerHome by Thomas R Clark
979-8838185136
The Ridge by Jeffery X Martin
979-8354516568
Through the Mist and the Madness: An Analytical Thesis on the First Three Metallica Albums by Jerome Reuter
979-8354143696
Like a Ton of Bricks by Paul Lubaczewski
979-8367912081
The Flock by Jeffery X Martin
979-8365780941

www.ingramcontent.com/pod-product-compliance
Lightning Source LLC
Chambersburg PA
CBHW020446220526
45464CB00002B/880